IF EXTINCT BEASTS CAME TO LIFE

PREHISTORIC
GIANTS

Thanks to the creative team:
Senior Editor: Alice Peebles
Consultant: Neil Clark
Fact Checker: Kate Mitchell
Design: www.collaborate.agency

Hungry Tomato™
A division of Lerner Publishing Group, Inc.
241 First Avenue North
Minneapolis, MN 55401 USA

For reading levels and more information, look up this title
at www.lernerbooks.com.

Main body text set in Franklin Gothic Book 11/12.
Typeface provided by International Typeface Corp.

Library of Congress Cataloging-in-Publication Data

Names: Rake, Matthew, author. | Mendez, Simon,
illustrator.
Title: Prehistoric giants / Matthew Rake ; illustrated by
Simon Mendez.
Description: Minneapolis : Hungry Tomato, [2017] |
Series: If extinct beasts came to life | Audience: Ages
8–12. | Audience: Grades 4 to 6. | Includes index.
Identifiers: LCCN 2016026384 (print) | LCCN
2016029202 (ebook) | ISBN 9781512406351 (lb : alk.
paper) | ISBN 9781512411614 (pb : alk. paper) | ISBN
9781512409123 (eb pdf)
Subjects: LCSH: Animals, Fossil—Juvenile literature. |
CYAC: Prehistoric animals.
Classification: LCC QE765 .R35 2017 (print) | LCC
QE765 (ebook) | DDC 560—dc23

LC record available at https://lccn.loc.gov/2016026384

Manufactured in the United States of America
1-39308-21145-8/31/2016

IF EXTINCT BEASTS CAME TO LIFE

PREHISTORIC GIANTS

by Matthew Rake
Illustrated by Simon Mendez

HUNGRY
TOMATO.

WARNING!
These extinct beasts
are not alive today, and
the encounters seen in
this book are not real.
But just imagine if
they were . . .

CONTENTS

THE BIG, THE BAD, AND THE UGLY

We all know dinosaurs reached ginormous proportions. But they weren't the only colossal creatures to roam the world before humans. Read on to discover some of the biggest, baddest, and ugliest animals ever to inhabit the planet.

Opabinia

So how did these creatures evolve? Well, all life started in the sea—and around 545 million years ago, many different animals began to appear. Some of them were truly weird. Take *Opabinia* (*left*). It had five mushroom-shaped eyes, fifteen body segments, and a grasping claw at the end of a long nose (or proboscis, to give it its scientific name). It used the proboscis to feed itself, like the elephant uses its trunk.

Out of the water, things got just as bizarre. About 300 million years ago, huge dragonflies took to the air. They had wingspans stretching to 26 inches (65 centimeters)—the same size as some of today's birds of prey. And massive millipedes—up to 7 feet, 6 inches (2.3 meters) long—marched across the land. It sounds like science fiction, but these creatures really existed!

The first dinosaurs evolved about 230–240 million years ago, but they didn't rule the world right away. Most, like *Compsognathus* (*left*), were only the size of turkeys. But they were fast, and they preyed on tiny reptiles and mammals that scampered around the forests. Over about 40 million years, dinosaurs became massive for various reasons, including an incredible abundance of food.

Compsognathus with prey

Mammals started evolving at the same time as dinosaurs. For about 160 million years, however, most mammals were shrew-sized—any larger and they would have been gobbled up by hungry carnivorous dinosaurs.

After the dinosaurs died out, mammals, such as the giant sloth *Megatherium* (*below*), grew to enormous proportions. You might think today's gorillas, elephants, camels, and rhinos are big— but they would all be dwarfed by their prehistoric ancestors. And even those creatures looked small compared to the biggest land mammal of all time— *Paraceratherium* (*left*).

What if these animals came back to life and and lived in the modern world? Read on to witness what an invasion from a prehistoric world would be like . . .

Paraceratherium

...and get ready for some bizarre and scary encounters between modern creatures and prehistoric beasts.

Megatherium

HEAD-BUTTING BEAST
MOSCHOPS

These days, there are people who earn money by walking dogs. It sounds like a nice job, with lots of fresh air and exercise. But surely this dog walker should be getting paid extra? After all, look at that beast she has to deal with. It's a *Moschops*, a massive mammal-like reptile that lived before the age of the dinosaurs. And, with that big, barrel-shaped body on top of those short legs, it doesn't look as if it wants to go anywhere fast.

Trying to encourage it to get a move on might not be the wisest move. *Moschops*'s skull was up to 4 inches (10 cm) thick—that's the width of a brick! It used it to head-butt rival *Moschops*, and some scientists even think they got on their hind legs to fight, like sumo wrestlers. So if this *Moschops* wants go at its own pace, the dog walker should let it!

MOSCHOPS

PRONOUNCED
MOSS-chops

LIVED
Forests of
South Africa,
267 million–260 million
years ago

LENGTH
About 9 feet (2.7 m)

WEIGHT
About 2,000 pounds
(914 kilograms)

TV STAR

In the 1980s, a *Moschops* was the star of an animated TV series of that name. The show also featured his friend Ally, an *Allosaurus*, grandfather *Diplodocus,* and Uncle Rex (yes, a *T. rex*). It wasn't exactly accurate. All those animals actually lived millions and millions of years apart!

HORNED HORROR
ESTEMMENOSUCHUS

So what on Earth is this crazy-looking creature? Is it a rhino? A hippo? A combination of the two? No, it's an *Estemmenosuchus*. And it's not some sort of dinosaur either—this mammal-like reptile lived about 25 million years before the first dinosaurs came along.

Don't worry—if *Estemmenosuchus* looks like a confusing creature to you, it is for scientists, too. They can't figure out whether it was a carnivore (meat-eater) or a herbivore (plant-eater). Its sharp canine and incisor teeth look as if they were made for ripping into flesh. But its big body seems made for digesting plant matter. And its short, widely set front legs are perfect for lowering its head to the ground to graze on plants. Maybe it's an omnivore, meaning it ate both meat and plants.

Whatever the answer, it doesn't look as if it will back down from this stand off with a lion. It might not be the speediest of animals, but with its huge horns and beefy body, it can probably look after itself. Its skull alone, at 26 inches (65 cm), is twice the length of the lion's. The king of the jungle might just have a rival for its crown.

ESTEMMENOSUCHUS
PRONOUNCED
Ess-tim-en-oh-SUE-kuss

LIVED
Russia, about 267 million years ago

LENGTH
Up to 15 feet (4.6 m)

WEIGHT
About 990 pounds (450 kg)

HEY, GOOD-LOOKIN'

The horns of *Estemmenosuchus* grew up and out from the skull bones and were probably designed for attracting mates, just as a peacock's feathers attract peahens.

BIG BEAST IN THE BIG APPLE
PARACERATHERIUM

OK, what's the world's largest land mammal? An elephant? That's right if we are talking about the modern world. But the largest land mammal of all time was *Paraceratherium*. It weighed four times more than an African elephant and was twice as tall. And it looks like it's just come back from the dead!

Don't worry, no one's directly in danger here. *Paraceratherium* was a herbivore, so it's probably looking for a park with a few trees to snack on. The pedestrians just need to make sure they don't get caught under its feet because it doesn't look like the nimblest of creatures. For the best (and safest) view, they probably should go inside a building—preferably three flights up for a great face-to-face encounter!

Paraceratherium is closely related to the rhino, but it lived like a giraffe, using its great height to feed on the tasty leaves out of reach of other animals. Scientists think it used its big incisor teeth to hold the branches and its big muscular lips to rip off the leaves.

PARACERATHERIUM

PRONOUNCED
Para-sera-THEE-rium

LIVED
Asia,
34 million–23 million
years ago

HEIGHT
16 feet (5 m) at the
shoulder

LENGTH
26 feet (8 m)

WEIGHT
16.5–22 tons
(15–20 metric tons)

HEAVIEST MAMMAL

Paraceratherium might be the heaviest ever land mammal, but it can't compare with the blue whale, the heaviest mammal of all. At about 200 tons (180 metric tons), the blue whale is 10 times heavier—and it is still around today, despite being hunted almost to extinction in the twentieth century.

TITANIC TURTLE
STUPENDEMYS

You'd probably think that the massive turtle *Stupendemys* would have been safe from predators 10 million years ago, when it lived in the waters of what became the Amazon River. Surely no other animal would have taken on this Titan with its supersized, shield-like shell. But *Stupendemys* lived at the same time as some of the biggest crocodiles ever to lurk in Earth's watery places. *Purusaurus*, for instance, could grow to a massive 42 feet (13 m) long, weighed around 9 tons (8.5 metric tons), and probably would have made short work of *Stupendemys*.

However, *Stupendemys* doesn't have much to worry about here in the Everglades of Florida. It can take a relaxing dip in the swamp waters safe in the knowledge that even the largest alligators, at 13 feet (4 m), are not going to do much damage to that shell.

STUPENDEMYS
PRONOUNCED
Stoo-PEND-ee-miss

LIVED
Northern South America,
10 million–5 million years ago

SHELL LENGTH
About 10 feet (3 m)

WEIGHT
About 1.6 tons
(1.5 metric tons)

UNDERWATER EATER
Stupendemys wasn't the only giant turtle to prowl around the Amazon in days gone by. *Carbonemys* lived about 50 million years earlier. Its shell was about 5 feet, 6 inches (1.7 m) long, and it had strong jaws that could eat small crocodiles.

BEETLE ON A TURTLE

Stupendemys was so large that you could easily have placed a Volkswagen Beetle on its shell. The animal was so heavy that scientists think it was probably a poor swimmer and spent most of its time chilling underwater and grazing on underwater plants.

MONKEY BUSINESS
GIGANTOPITHECUS

Who is this unexpected visitor to the Great Wall of China? Meet *Gigantopithecus*, the biggest ape ever to walk the Earth. It's twice the height of a gorilla and three times its weight—but, even so, it's not a danger to these sightseers. By studying its teeth and jaws, scientists have discovered that *Gigantopithecus* liked a diet of fruit, nuts, and shoots. Some scientists think it might have gobbled up the occasional small mammal or lizard, but only as a side dish.

Although *Gigantopithecus* might look like a gorilla, its closest living relative is actually the orangutan. Like the orangutan, Gigantopithecus lived in forests—but it found it harder and harder to find food when, around 100,000 years ago, the climate began to get cooler and forests started shrinking. And of course, unlike the orangutan, it would have missed out on all the fruit growing in the treetops. It might be able to climb the Great Wall of China, but it was far too heavy to climb trees!

GIGANTOPITHECUS
PRONOUNCED
Jye-GAN-toe-PITH-
eh-kuss
LIVED
China, India,
Vietnam, and Nepal,
9 million–100,000
years ago
LENGTH
10 feet (3 m)
WEIGHT
1,190 pounds (540 kg)

MYSTERY BEAST
Scientists have found more than one thousand fossilized teeth of *Gigantopithecus* and some of its jaw bones— but no fossils of its lower body. So no one is exactly sure what this beast looked like.

RUNAWAY RHINO
ELASMOTHERIUM

Every July charging bulls, led by human runners, are let loose on the streets of Pamplona in Spain. And they cause complete havoc. Running at an average speed of 15 miles per hour (24 kilometers per hour), the bulls usually injure between fifty and one hundred people. Those who slip or are pushed over are the lucky ones—you just want to avoid being gored by those horns!

This year, things have become a whole lot more dangerous because look what joined the fun: an *Elasmotherium*. That's a giant rhino to you and me. These creatures were the size of elephants—about 4.4 tons (4 metric tons) of solid flesh, bone, and muscle. They were covered in hair, and scientists think they galloped like horses. What's more, while bulls' horns seem dangerous, check out *Elasmotherium*'s. Now the bulls might be in as much danger as the runners . . .

MISSING HORNS

Elasmotherium's horn was made from keratin—the same substance that makes up human hair and fingernails. Unfortunately, keratin doesn't fossilize well, so nobody knows the exact length of the horn. But scientists think it was about 5 feet, 9 inches (1.75 m) long.

ELASMOTHERIUM
PRONOUNCED
Eh-laz-moe-THEE-ree-um

LIVED
Plains of Asia and
Eastern Europe,
2 million–30,000
years ago

LENGTH
20 feet (6 m)

WEIGHT
3.3–4.4 tons
(3-4 metric tons)

HEIGHT
6 feet, 6 inches (2 m)

NEW KNOWLEDGE

In 2016, new research on a piece of *Elasmotherium* skull found in Kazakhstan showed that the animal lived until about 30,000 years ago. Previously scientists thought it had died out 350,000 years ago. This means the creature lived at the same time as humans.

MAGNIFICENT MARSUPIAL
DIPROTODON

Looks like we have an extra player for the volleyball match. We're not sure that this pigeon-toed creature is going to be the best teammate though. It doesn't look like it can make the sharpest moves or react very quickly.

So who—or what—is this new player? It's a *Diprotodon,* and it lived in Australia until 40,000 years ago. Like Australia's kangaroo and koala, it was a marsupial, which means it kept its young in a pouch. Some people think *Diprotodon* looks a little like the koala. Perhaps, but only if you imagine the koala to be the size of a hippopotamus and fully capable of crunching a human skull between its two back molars! *Diprotodon* was a plant-eater—but hippos are also vegetarians, and that hasn't stopped them from killing people. So maybe the players should take a time-out and chill with an ice cream cone until their court is *Diprotodon*-free!

DIPROTODON
PRONOUNCED
Dye-PRO-toe-don
LIVED
Australia,
1.8 million–40,000
years ago
LENGTH
Up to 13 feet (4 m)
WEIGHT
Up to 3.3 tons
(3 metric tons)

REAR VIEW

Diprotodon's pouch faced backward, so the baby's view of the world would have been framed by its mother's hind legs! The modern Australian wombat also has a backward-facing pouch. When it digs, soil doesn't get in the pouch!

GIANT SLOTH
MEGATHERIUM

These days, sloths live in trees in South America and weigh 13 pounds (6 kg) at most. That's less than a Jack Russell terrier. *Megatherium*, however, wouldn't last long in a tree—and the tree wouldn't last too long either! It weighed 4.4 tons (4 metric tons)—about the same as an elephant!

As you can see, this giant sloth could reach leaves in the treetops simply by standing on its hind legs. In this position, it stood as tall as a modern giraffe. To get at any leaves still out of reach, it could use its large claws and powerful arms to pull branches down to its mouth. Scientists think *Megatherium* also had a long, strong tongue that it wrapped around the branches to strip off leaves and fresh growth. And if there were no trees to feed on? Then it would use its big claws to dig at plant roots. And it looks like there are lots of plants in this yard to try!

MEGATHERIUM
PRONOUNCED
Meg-ah-THEE-ree-um
LIVED
South America,
2 million–10,000
years ago
LENGTH
20 feet (6 m)
WEIGHT
4.4 tons (4 metric tons)

KILLER CLAWS?
Megatherium's huge claws measured almost 12 inches (30 cm) long and prevented it from putting its feet flat on the ground—it had to walk on the sides of its feet. Some scientists have even claimed that *Megatherium* used its claws to slash and kill other animals. They think it ate meat as well as plants.

CLIMB OR DIG?
Frenchman Georges Cuvier was the first to identify the giant sloth, in 1796. He thought its huge claws were used for climbing trees. Then he changed his mind—probably when he realized it was too big to climb trees! He decided the sloth must have lived underground and used its claws to dig tunnels.

TOWERING CAMEL
TITANOTYLOPUS

There is only one winner in this camel race, and it's the giant camel *Titanotylopus*. Just look at those legs go. *Titanotylopus* was twice the height of modern camels. Its legs alone are taller than that jockey! There are a few questions you have to ask about this race though. For a start, how did the jockey get on *Titanotylopus*? A stepladder? And, more importantly, how will he stay on? It looks like it's going to be a bumpy ride!

Titanotylopus remains have been found across the United States—including in Texas, Kansas, and Arizona. But giant camel fossils have also been found in the Arctic! Yes, that's right—about 3.4 million years ago, camels lived on Ellesmere Island in Canada, opposite Greenland, in one of the world's coldest, bleakest spots. This camel—known as the High Arctic camel—wasn't as big as *Titanotylopus,* but it was still much bigger than modern camels.

TITANOTYLOPUS
PRONOUNCED
Tie-tan-oh-TIE-low-puss
LIVED
Plains of North America, Europe, and Asia, 5 million–300,000 years ago
LENGTH
13 feet (4 m)
WEIGHT
1.1–2.2 tons (1–2 metric tons)

ARCTIC DRIFTER
The High Arctic camel was well-adapted for life in the cold. Its wide, flat feet enabled it to walk on snow, and as in the desert, it could live off energy stored in its hump.

KING OF THE GRASSLANDS
MAMMOTH

This is what we call a real stand-off: monster fire truck versus, er, monster. This is a Steppe mammoth, the largest mammoth that ever existed. It weighed twice as much as the largest elephant, and its tusks were 16 feet (5 m) long.

You think this stand-off is just fantasy? Don't be so sure. In May 2013, on the island of Maly Lyakhovsky, north of Russia, a mammoth was found buried in the frozen ground. It had been eaten alive by wolves while stuck in a peat bog. Despite this grisly attack, most of its body parts were intact—including three legs, most of its body, and even its trunk. Its blood had also frozen—and from this, scientists are hoping to get DNA to clone a new mammoth. So maybe, in the future, the world really could be like the movie *Jurassic Park,* and stand offs like this will be common.

MAMMOTH
LIVED
Europe and Asia,
5 million years ago–
1,650 BCE

HEIGHT
Up to 13 feet (4 m)
at the shoulder

WEIGHT
11–16.5 tons
(10–15 metric tons)

DIAL 911

END OF AN ERA

Why did mammoths die out?
Some scientists think that when the
Ice Age ended, around 12,000 years
ago, mammoths lost their habitat,
as open grasslands and woodlands
were replaced by forests. Others
think the animals were hunted to
extinction by humans. Perhaps both
these factors, combined with rising
sea levels, brought about the end of
these majestic beasts.

TIMELINE

ESTEMMENOSUCHUS

Named after the Greek for "crowned crocodile"

Estemmenosuchus belonged to the therapsid group of reptiles from which mammals evolved. Therapsids had three kinds of teeth: incisors in front, stabbing canines, and molars for grinding.

PARACERATHERIUM

Named after the Greek for "near the hornless beast"

Paraceratherium, first discovered in 1907–1908, was named because it looked like *Aceratherium*, another rhino-like creature, whose name means—yes, you guessed it—"hornless beast."

STUPENDEMYS

Named after the Greek for "astonishing turtle"

The earliest turtle evolved around 220 million years ago. When the dinosaurs died out about 66 million years ago, turtles survived because they could live on very little for a long time.

MOSCHOPS

Named after the Greek for "calf face"

Moschops was a therapsid too. It also had a 4-inch-thick (10 cm) skull, so that didn't leave much room for the brain.

GIGANTOPITHECUS

Named after the Greek for "giant ape"

The first time that the existence of *Gigantopithecus* came to light was in 1935, when paleontologist Ralph von Koenigswald found an extremely large fossilized molar tooth in an apothecary shop in Hong Kong! (In China, old animal teeth are called dragons' teeth. They are used in traditional medicine.)

267 MILLION YEARS AGO ▷ Around 230 million years ago: First dinosaurs evolve ▷ 66 million years ago: End of the dinosaurs ▷ ▷

ELASMOTHERIUM

Named after the Greek for "thin plate beast"

When fossils from this giant one-horned beast were first discovered in Siberia, they were thought to belong to the mythical unicorn. Stories were told of its horn being so large that it had to be transported by sled. *Elasmotherium* is still informally known as the Siberian unicorn.

MAMMOTH

Derived from *mamant*, meaning "Earth-horn" in the Mansi language of Russia

Steppe mammoths lived on the plains of Europe and Asia. To fuel their huge bodies, they ground up large amounts of grasses with their broad teeth.

DIPROTODON

Named after the Greek for "two forward teeth"

In 2009–2012, scientists found fifty *Diprotodons* in Queensland, Australia. The animals may have become trapped while searching for water. Teeth from crocodiles and lizards at the site suggest they were eaten alive by these reptiles.

TITANOTYLOPUS

Named after the Greek for "knobby foot"

Camels originated in North America about 40 million years ago. They reached Asia across the Bering Strait, which used to be dry land between Alaska and Russia. They eventually made it to the Middle East and North Africa.

MEGATHERIUM

Named after the Greek for "great beast"

Megatherium tracks left on the ground—as well as its bones—have been fossilized. These prove that it walked on both two feet and all fours.

UNCOVERING THE PAST

Without the careful and dedicated work of paleontologists, we would know nothing about our prehistoric past. These scientists search for fossils, the remains of extinct animals, to identify and understand early life forms.

A body fossil is an actual part of an animal, such as teeth or bones, preserved in rock. Fossils of the same animal can be discovered in different places. The first fossils found of the largest land mammal, *Paraceratherium* (*above and page 12*), were discovered in Balochistan, Pakistan, in 1907–1908 by the British geologist Guy Ellcock Pilgrim. Others have since been found in Kazakhstan, China, and Mongolia.

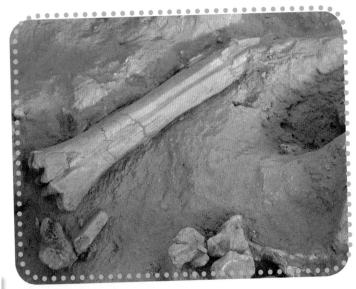

No matter how mighty the original animal was, fossils of its body parts can be very delicate and need to be wrapped up carefully. When scientists tried to move the first fossils of *Paraceratherium*, many of them shattered. Remember, there weren't nice roads and modern cars in those days—most transportation was done by camel!

CRYPTIDS

Paraceratherium was a genuine discovery. Cryptids, on the other hand, are animals that people claim to have seen, but for which there is no scientific proof of existence. For example, Big Foot is a large, hairy ape that supposedly lives in the forests of the northwestern United States, similar to the Yeti of the Himalayan mountains. And, of course, there is the Loch Ness monster (*artist's impression, right*), first "sighted" lurking in its Scottish loch (lake) in 1933. But a famous photograph of it, supposedly taken the following year, has been proved to be a fake. The monster's head and neck were out of the water, and the ripples on the water are completely out of proportion to them!

Even so, some people do think Nessie exists and is a plesiosaur: a giant, long-necked sea reptile from the time of the dinosaurs. Others have even claimed it is a sauropod, a long-necked dinosaur. Although why a land-dwelling dinosaur is living in a loch is anyone's guess! Also, Loch Ness was formed about 10,000 years ago—and plesiosaurs and sauropods lived more than 66 million years ago!

Extinction

Until the nineteenth century, most people did not think animals went extinct. When a fossil of an unknown animal was found, experts thought it must live in an unexplored part of the world. But now everyone knows that animals become extinct, often because humans hunted them.

In North America, the saber-toothed tiger and the mammoth went extinct at around the time humans arrived. More recent extinctions include the elephant bird of Madagascar and the dodo (*right*), a flightless bird from the island of Mauritius. Both birds died out around the seventeenth century. The dodo died out less than 100 years after the first humans settled on Mauritius.

31

INDEX

The Author

Matthew Rake lives in London, in the United Kingdom, and has worked in publishing for more than twenty years. He has written on a wide variety of topics for adults as well as children, including science, sports, and the arts.

The Illustrator

Award-winning illustrator Simon Mendez combines his love of nature and drawing by working as an illustrator with a focus on scientific and natural subjects. He paints on a wide variety of themes but mainly concentrates on portraits and animal subjects. He lives in the United Kingdom.

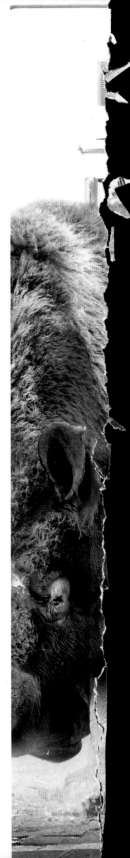